Iron
and
Steel

STEEL

FROM THOR'S HAMMER TO
THE SPACE SHUTTLE

RUTH G. KASSINGER

Material World

Twenty-First Century Books
Brookfield, Connecticut

In memory of Dr. Burton I. Edelson

Library of Congress Cataloging-in-Publication Data
Kassinger, Ruth, 1954–
Iron and steel : from Thor's hammer to the space shuttle / Ruth G. Kassinger.
p. cm. — (Material world)
Summary: A discussion of iron and steel which includes a scientific description of these met-
als, their discovery, and their uses throughout history and in the present. Includes a time-
line. Includes bibliographical references and index.
ISBN 0-7613-2111-X (lib. bdg.)
1. Iron—Juvenile literature. 2. Steel—Juvenile literature. [1. Iron. 2. Steel.] I. Title.
II. Series: Kassinger, Ruth, 1954
TN705.K28 2003   669'.1—dc21   2002011516

An Iron Age votive chariot

Published by Twenty-First Century Books
A Division of The Millbrook Press, Inc.
2 Old New Milford Road
Brookfield, Connecticut 06804
www.millbrookpress.com

Contents

This beautiful stag made of bronze and gold was found in the royal tombs of a town near Hattusa in modern Turkey and was made before 2000 B.C.

CHAPTER ONE
The Birth of Iron

HATTUSA

On the top of a windswept rocky hill in the central plain of modern Turkey are the remnants of one of the ancient world's greatest cities, Hattusa, capital of the Hittite empire. When the empire was at the height of its power in about 1350 B.C., a massive stone wall 4 miles (6.4 kilometers) long and as much as 26 feet (8 meters) wide circled the city. Inside the wall, on a towering cliff, stood the Great Palace of the Hittite kings, which looked down on the inhabitants' mud-brick houses below.

Inside the palace were many rooms. Some were for worship of the Hittites' dozens of gods, and some were for living. A huge hall occupied the entire second floor. Conquered leaders assembled there to offer their gifts of gold, purple cloth, oil, and jewels to the Hittite king and to acknowledge that they were his subjects. There were also rooms full of baked clay tablets that scribes had etched with treaties, tax receipts, and other important information. And there were row upon row of rooms where the gifts from foreigners, as well as treasures made by the Hittite people, were kept safe.

The mountains near Hattusa were rich in gold and silver deposits as well as copper *ore* (rock that contains a valuable metal). Hittite metalworkers became expert at shaping gold and silver as well as bronze—which is an alloy (combination) of copper and tin. The treasure rooms of the Great Palace and other royal residences held beautiful goblets, plates, small statues, jewelry, and other objects made from these precious metals.

The mountains near Hattusa also held iron ore, which the Hittites mined to obtain *iron*, a heavy metal that rusts easily and is malleable. Hittite craftsmen used iron to make weapons even more valuable than the gold, silver, copper, and bronze treasures. These iron swords and daggers weren't beautiful, and they didn't shine like the bronze weapons that people from other nations used, but some of the iron weapons made by Hittite *blacksmiths* (people who worked iron into objects) were sharper and their edges didn't dull as quickly. They were stored like the other Hittite treasures in the palace storerooms.

Some historians believe that the Hittites' success in conquering other nations in the Near East was due to the superiority of their iron weapons.

By the time the Hittites began making their secret iron in about 1400 B.C., people had been smelting copper from copper ore for 2,000 years. Copper is beautiful, but it is a soft metal. It made lovely jewelry and could be used for cups, plates, bowls, and some pots, but it was too soft for most tools and weapons. By 3000 B.C., people had learned to melt copper and tin together to make the much-harder bronze. Coppersmiths discovered that if they added a little iron ore to the copper and tin ore in their furnaces, it would lower the temperature at which the metals melted. It was probably by accident, therefore, that they made iron bloom.

Certainly, people from Assyria and Babylonia to the east and as far away as Egypt to the south were eager to trade their goods for the Hittites' iron and iron weapons.

Iron ore is a common material around the world and can be found in many of the countries that bought iron and iron weapons from the Hittites. And by 1400 B.C., coppersmiths (people who shaped copper into objects) in several areas of the Near East had managed to *smelt* (separate by heating) iron from iron ore in the furnaces they used to smelt copper from its ore. So why did these people want the Hittites' iron? The answer is simple. They hadn't learned the secret of making objects out of iron.

When iron ore was smelted at the relatively low temperatures that smiths achieved in copper smelting furnaces, the iron didn't run out from the ore as a liquid as copper did. It emerged from the furnace in lumpy pieces of a metal and rock mixture that we call *bloom*. The coppersmiths would then wait until the bloom cooled before hammering it, just as they did with copper, but when they hammered cold bloom, it often broke. Even when they succeeded in shaping a dagger, the dagger was no sharper than the bronze ones they made more easily. And unlike bronze daggers, iron daggers rusted.

THE SECRETS OF THE HITTITES

The Hittites, on the other hand, discovered that if they heated the bloom until it was red-hot and then hammered it, it wouldn't break. In fact, they found that when they hammered the red-hot bloom, the bits of iron separated from the rocky mass and

This is a Hittite dagger-sword made of *iron about 1100* B.C. *Much of it has turned to rust over the past three thousand years.*

became *welded* (joined by means of heating) to each other. The hammering forced out most of the rocky mass (*slag*). After many rounds of heating and hammering, the Hittites found they could hammer the iron into useful objects. Iron that has been repeatedly heated to red-hot temperatures and hammered is called *wrought iron.*

Wrought iron could be formed into a huge variety of shapes, from buttons to weapons. It still rusted and couldn't be poured into molds as copper and bronze could. On the other hand, iron ore was plentiful. Moreover, it appears that in the Near East between 1400 and 1200 B.C., there was a great shortage of the tin needed to make bronze. There were few tin deposits in the Near East, and wars reduced or eliminated tin imports. The Hittites' wrought iron became a valuable substitute for bronze, which was in short supply.

In addition, the Hittite blacksmiths discovered another secret about iron that allowed them to make a special iron that was even harder and stronger and more valuable than their wrought iron. Archaeologists (scientists who study ancient human cultures by studying the tools, pottery, and other relics of those societies) have uncovered a clay tablet letter written by a Hittite king in the thirteenth century B.C. to a king of Assyria that reads:

> As for the good iron which you wrote about to me. Good iron is not available in my seal house in Kizzuwatna. That it is a bad time for producing iron, I have written. They will produce good iron, but as yet they will not have finished. When they have finished I shall send it to you. Today, now, I am dispatching an iron dagger blade to you.

Archaeologists and historians believe that the "good iron" that the king wrote about was actually iron that had been worked in a way that gave it a harder exterior layer. Ordinary wrought iron is no harder or more capable of making a sharp edge than bronze. But when hot iron combines with a small amount of carbon (about 1 percent), it becomes *carburized* and is then steel. *Steel* is harder than bronze and makes better weapons. Some, but not all, of the Hittite iron was the "good iron" (steel) that the Assyrian king particularly wanted.

Archaeologists now believe that the Hittites accidentally invented steel as they made wrought iron. Sometimes when a blacksmith reheated the iron to red-hot temperatures, he would leave it in the furnace nestled in the glowing charcoal. If the iron rested long enough on burning charcoal that was hot enough, a little of the carbon from the charcoal would enter the surface of the iron. The surface layer of the iron became steel. Because blacksmiths didn't understand why wrought iron sometimes became harder than usual, they weren't able—as the Hittite king's letter indicates—to produce "good iron" consistently. When they did, though, it was very valuable.

IRON TAKES OVER

The Hittites kept the secrets of wrought iron and iron with a surface of steel for about two hundred years. But about 1200 B.C., the Hittite empire collapsed. No one knows exactly what happened, but it seems likely that invaders either from the eastern Mediterranean or from Thrace and Phrygia to the northwest invaded and conquered. The invaders burned Hattusa to the ground and drove the inhabitants into exile in foreign lands.

Some of the exiles must have been blacksmiths who carried their iron-making secrets with them. Before long, the technology of iron making spread throughout the Near East. By 1000 B.C., iron had replaced bronze as the most popular metal for making tools and weapons in the Near East. The Near Eastern Iron Age had begun.

Iron-making technology spread westward to Europe, too. Traders from the Near East brought gems, jewelry, wine, and oil to exchange for metals, salt, and amber (a hard yellow resin used to make jewelry) from the West. Ideas were exchanged as well as goods, and by 700 B.C. the secret of iron making had spread throughout central Europe. The European Iron Age had begun.

NEW TECHNOLOGIES

As new people learned iron-making technology, some made improvements upon it. Sometime around 1000 B.C., black-

This modern-day blacksmith is hammering
a piece of red-hot iron, much like a Hittite blacksmith
might have thousands of years ago.

smiths in the Near East found that they could make a piece of carburized iron even harder if they cooled it suddenly by plunging it into water, a technique now known as *quenching*. Among the European tribes that adopted quenched-steel technology were the Celts. The Celts were a rough but energetic and creative people who used the new technology to make sharp steel swords that they used to defeat other European tribes who hadn't adopted the technology. They also invented *chain mail*, which was body armor made of small iron rings linked together and fashioned into a kind of shirt. With their armor and armaments of iron, by about 500 B.C. the Celts had conquered most of Europe.

The Celts also used iron and steel for peaceful purposes, fashioning iron shoes for horses, making iron plows, rimming their wagon wheels with iron, and inventing all kinds of tools, such as chisels and saws, that we still use today. But iron did not yet change ordinary Europeans' lives dramatically. Iron was a good replacement for bronze, but it was still expensive. Although iron ore was readily available in many places, it took

The pulley above and these other Iron Age tools took European blacksmiths many hours to make.

an enormous amount of labor to smelt iron from it and *forge* it (hammer it into shape). The average peasant had few iron implements.

The Romans made an additional discovery about iron in the fourth century B.C. They found that if they reheated quenched steel to about 1300°F (700°C) for a short time, it lost some of its brittleness (although it also lost a little sharpness). This process was called *tempering* and was the third improvement, after carburization and quenching, that turned a useful product, wrought iron, into more valuable steel. Plows made of quenched and tempered steel were less likely to break when they hit a rock. Steel tools were expensive, so each improvement made it more likely that a craftsman would purchase and use one.

Although iron ore was plentiful and steel was a wonderful material, it took lots of effort to make steel tools and weapons. Blacksmiths had to continually pump air into their furnaces with *bellows* (accordionlike devices that push air onto the flames to make the furnace hotter) in order to keep their furnace hot enough long enough to smelt iron. They had no thermometers to help them judge the temperature of the fire. After the smelting, it took hours of hard physical labor—hammering, reheating, hammering, quenching, and tempering—to shape iron bloom into a steel-surfaced object. Tempering was an especially delicate operation, and mistakes could ruin days of effort.

No doubt there were blacksmiths who wished that iron was a material like copper and bronze that could be melted in a

Blacksmiths in this fifteenth-century Italian fresco by an anonymous artist are using a forge to hammer iron into a useful shape. Forges like this had been used since ancient times.

furnace and then *cast* (poured) into molds. It is far easier to pour a liquid metal into a mold than to hammer it into a shape. But iron doesn't melt until it reaches 2800°F (1537°C), and European and Near Eastern blacksmiths were unable to raise the temperature in their furnaces that high. It was the Chinese who were first able to do this.

CHINESE INNOVATIONS

There was no iron making in China until the technology for making wrought iron came from the Near East hundreds of years after the fall of the Hittite empire. The earliest Chinese iron implement discovered by archaeologists is a wrought-iron dagger made about 650 B.C. Once the Chinese learned to make iron, however, they quickly became adept at smelting and forging wrought-iron tools and weapons.

This scene from a Chinese vase depicts blacksmiths at work.

The Chinese then took iron and steel making in a new direction in the next century. First, they invented a new kind of bellows that sent a continuous, large flow of air into the furnace. With these bellows, the Chinese were able to raise the temperature in their furnaces above the melting point (2800°F or 1537°C) of iron. Iron flowed like a liquid from the Chinese furnaces. Chinese iron makers could then pour liquid iron into molds. This was the answer to blacksmiths' dreams: iron that could be cast as easily as copper and bronze!

Unfortunately, this *cast iron* had too much carbon in it (about 5 percent). When iron has this much carbon, it is very hard but also very brittle. It meant that a cast-iron pot might shatter when struck with a spoon. A dagger of cast iron would be too fragile to use.

Fortunately, the Chinese made a second discovery. They discovered a way to give their cast iron a tough steel surface. They found that when they reheated a cast-iron object to about 1560°F (850°C), some of the oxygen in the air combined with carbon on the object's surface. (This process became known as *roasting*.) After a cast-iron object was roasted for some time, the level of carbon in its surface was reduced to about 1 percent—enough to make the surface of the object steel. The Chinese created cast iron that was as durable and tough as wrought iron that had been quenched and tempered. It would be a thousand years before the Europeans would catch up with these Chinese innovations.

Cast-iron making in China reached its peak there between 206 B.C. and A.D. 220. Archaeologists have unearthed huge furnaces that produced enough molten iron to cast many thousands of iron objects, including buckles, coins, shovels, hoes, and plows. If the blacksmiths had no immediate need for the iron, they poured it into oblong bars, which could be melted again later. Because it was so much easier and quicker to cast iron than to forge it, the Chinese made far greater use of iron than any other people of the period. Chinese farmers were far more likely to use iron tools than European farmers were.

INDIA

The secrets of making wrought iron passed from the Near East to the area that is today India and Pakistan. As early as 500 B.C., blacksmiths there had developed their own secret way of making steel. Their method produced only small amounts of steel at a time, but with it Indian blacksmiths made hard, yet flexible steel swords that were coveted around the world.

The Indian blacksmiths mixed plant leaves, pieces of wood, and small pieces of wrought iron in a small crucible (a container that can survive high heat). They then sealed the crucible with clay and buried it in a pit filled with white hot charcoal. Under the high heat, the carbon in the plant leaves and wood mixed with the iron and carburized all the iron, not just the surface iron. The iron that emerged was steel all the way through. This special, highly valuable steel was known as *wootz steel*. Indian blacksmiths kept the secret of wootz steel for hundreds of years.

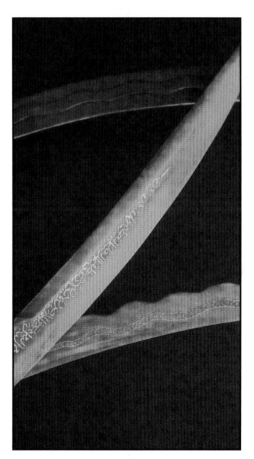

This sword blade is made of *wootz steel and inlaid with gold.*

CHAPTER TWO
Myth, Magic, and Iron and Steel

HEAVENLY IRON

Meteorites, masses made largely of iron, nickel, and other metals that arrive from outer space, have always amazed people. The friction of the metal against the gas molecules of the atmosphere makes them glow. Often meteorites burn up in the atmosphere, but sometimes (about two thousand times each year), they plunge to Earth. Blackened and extraordinarily hard and heavy, meteorites seemed to ancient people to be sent from heaven, and in some cultures they were worshiped as gods.

Before people learned to smelt iron, they managed to beat small pieces of meteorites into sacred objects, such as knives or medallions. Because the meteoric iron contained nickel, it made very strong swords and daggers. Beads made of meteoric iron were worn in Egypt as early as 4000 B.C.

The Sumerians, who prospered in what is modern Iraq from about 3500 to 2000 B.C., valued meteoric iron and attributed divine powers to it. Their word for iron, which is the world's oldest name for the metal, is formed from two pictograms (pictures used as symbols), one for "sky" and one for "fire."

The largest meteorite that has fallen to Earth (that we know of) landed in Grootfontein, Namibia, about 80,000 years ago. It is made of 82 percent iron, 16 percent nickel, 1 percent cobalt, and a trace of other metals. It is somewhat smaller in size than a small car, but weighs about sixty times as much. A small car weighs about 1 ton, and the meteorite weighs about 60 tons (54 metric tons)!

One of the world's most famous meteorites is the Hajar al Aswad, a black iron meteorite that landed in what is today Saudi Arabia. Ancient people must have felt that there was something magical about the meteorite because when they built a shrine (called the Kaaba) to their pagan gods, they built it into one of its walls. When the Muslim prophet Muhammad conquered Mecca in 630, he declared the Kaaba a sacred shrine to Allah and kissed the black stone embedded in its wall. Today, when devout Muslims travel to Mecca, they visit the Kaaba and touch or kiss the black stone as Muhammad did.

THE METAL OF THE GODS

In the first millennium B.C., as the Hittites' iron technology spread throughout the Near East and then slowly to the east and west, iron became the metal of choice for weaponry. Soldiers recognized the superiority of steel swords and daggers, which could pierce the bronze shields that until then had provided soldiers with excellent protection. Iron weapons must have made their owners feel very powerful. Iron's extraordinary hardness made it seem magical and fit for gods.

In Scandinavian mythology, the fiercest and mightiest god was Thor. He was charged with protecting all the other gods of Asgard, the home of the Scandinavian gods. Thor's weapon for fighting off the evil monsters, frost giants, and trolls who threatened to bring chaos to the world was an iron hammer.

In this Viking miniature,
Thor holds his iron hammer. Around
A.D. 1000, Viking men and women
often wore miniature Thor's hammers
around their necks. A person who
wore a hammer probably believed that
it would provide him or her with the
protection of Thor.

He also used the hammer, forged by a dwarf blacksmith, to create thunder and lightning. Thor's hammer was unbreakable, always struck its target, and always came back to him, no matter how hard and how far he threw it. In one myth, the gods are called upon to decide which of the magical objects made by the dwarves and elves was the most wonderful. The gods gave that honor to Thor's hammer. The myth reflects how much the Scandinavians valued iron.

In Greek mythology, Hephaestus was the god of iron, the forge, and crafts. Unlike Thor, Hephaestus was a gentle god who tried to make peace among his quarrelsome siblings and parents on Mount Olympus. The ancient Greeks imagined him as muscular but ugly, which is surely a reflection of the way they thought about iron itself—strong but unattractive. Hephaestus made decorative objects, cups, and bowls as well as armor for the gods and thunderbolts for Zeus, the chief Greek god. Iron, in the eyes of the Greeks, was as valuable for its peaceful uses as it was for its military uses.

Perhaps the most famous iron or steel sword in history is Excalibur, the magical sword of King Arthur. Historians think that the legendary Arthur may have been based on a Celtic chieftain who lived in England sometime between A.D. 450 and 650. During that era, the Romans retreated from England as the Germanic Angles and Saxons invaded. Whether Arthur was real or imaginary, by the ninth century he and his military feats were famous in Wales, the western part of Britain where the Celts found refuge after their defeat.

The legend of Arthur's unbeatable sword first appears in the fictional *History of the Kings of Britain*, written about 1130 by

The stories about magical iron swords evolved not only because carburized iron was stronger than bronze but because carburized iron swords varied greatly in quality. Some swords had too much carbon and were brittle; others had too little and were soft. But the rare sword with just the right amount of carbon and the finest hammering gave its owner the edge in battle and was highly valuable.

Geoffrey of Monmouth. The author imagines that Arthur conquered much of Scandinavia and then attacked Frollo, leader of the Gauls, in Paris. Arthur and Frollo meet in single combat, and Arthur smites Frollo on the head so hard with his sword that the Gaul's head is split in two. No armor can stand up to the sharp edge of Arthur's sword.

In later versions of the Arthur legend, Arthur's swords become more important. In Sir Thomas Malory's *Le Morte D'Arthur* (*The Death of Arthur*), printed in 1485, Arthur proves his noble birth by pulling out a sword that seems to be permanently stuck in a stone. That sword breaks, but he receives another invincible sword called Excalibur from the magical Lady of the Lake. Arthur uses Excalibur to defeat those who oppose him and his knights on their noble quest for the Holy Grail. When Arthur is dying, he asks one of his knights to throw the sword back in the lake, where a woman's white arm reaches out from the water to catch it and return it to its magical home.

THE EVIL IN IRON

While iron could be used for good, people were well aware that iron could be used for evil. The period between 1000 B.C. and 500 B.C., when iron superseded bronze in much of the western

The legend of Sir Arthur and Excalibur inspired art as well as literature. This painting by the Italian Giacomo Jaquerio is titled Arthur and Charlemagne.

25

An ancient Indian myth about iron reflects the feelings about the destructive capabilities of iron.

According to this myth, men used to work for Sing Bonga, the supreme god, in the heavens. After a time, though, men came to believe they were equal to Sing Bonga, and Sing Bonga flung them down to Earth. They landed in a place where they found iron ore, so they built furnaces to make iron and became blacksmiths.

Sing Bonga, irritated by the smoke the furnaces sent to heaven, caused the furnaces to disintegrate. Later he came to Earth disguised as an old man, and the blacksmiths asked him how to save the furnaces. "Offer a human sacrifice," he said, and demonstrated that when he went into the furnace, he came out with gold, silver, and jewels. The smiths eagerly followed suit and went into the furnaces while their wives operated the bellows. When the wives heard cries from inside, the old man said the sounds were just their husbands' happy shouts as they divided up the treasure. The wives kept firing the furnaces until the blacksmiths were reduced to ashes.

world, was a time of frequent wars and mass migrations. For people who lived by farming, war meant ruined crops and starvation. For many, iron was the metal of destruction.

In some ancient cultures, blacksmiths were admired for their knowledge and skill, as well as the great strength they had to have in order to hammer iron. Among African tribes that relied on farming as a way of life, the blacksmith was deeply respected because he was the one who made the iron plows, hoes, and other implements that farmers needed to do their work. But in African tribes that relied on herding and hunting, blacksmiths were often disliked. We can't be sure why this was so, but it is likely that these tribes encountered iron as implements of war, not of agriculture. They may also have been frightened by the unfamiliar fiery, smoky conditions of a blacksmith's forge.

LIVING IRON

The ancient Greeks were curious about the world around them. Although most Greeks believed their gods were directly responsible for natural events, some Greek philosophers looked for a different kind of understanding about nature. Men like the ancient Greek philosopher Aristotle (384–322 B.C.) turned to logic to explain the presence of different kinds of metals in the earth.

The Masai, of eastern Africa, relied on herding cattle not farming. They despised blacksmiths because their religion forbids bloodshed and smiths made weapons that caused bloodshed. They believed that entering the area where a blacksmith lived and worked could bring death or disease. The daughters of blacksmiths were not wanted as wives because, it was thought, they could bring death to their husbands or bear sickly children.

Aristotle was a great observer of nature and drew conclusions about how the world works from his observations. One phenomenon that Aristotle noticed was that immature (and in Aristotle's view, valueless) beings grew into mature (valuable) beings. For example, useless seeds grew into edible plants, helpless lambs grew into wool-bearing sheep, and unreasoning babies grew into rational adults. Aristotle generalized from his observations and concluded that all things in this world—plants, animals, and people—grow toward perfection.

Aristotle thought his observation applied to metals, too. He noticed that there were large amounts of unattractive metals in the ground, such as iron, lead, and tin. Copper, an attractive metal, was harder to find than these other, uglier metals. Silver was rarer still. Because gold never dulled while copper corroded and silver tarnished, and because gold was the least abundant metal of these three, Aristotle concluded that base metals grew by stages into gold. Copper and silver, he believed, were still in the process of maturing into gold.

Odd as the ancient Greek theory seems to us today, it was convincing to many people until only a few hundred years ago. Ancient miners often blocked the entrance to mines to allow Earth to grow more metals or minerals in her "womb." One French historian, Bernard Palissy, wrote in 1563 that the Earth produced metals the same way as soil produced crops. As late as the seventeenth century, the distinguished German chemist Johann Glauber wrote that if a metal reached perfection and was not extracted from the Earth, it would deteriorate much as animals do when they grow old. It wasn't until the eighteenth century that the notion that metals were alive finally died.

When the Greeks conquered Egypt in 332 B.C., they spread the belief to Egypt that metals like iron would grow, eventually, into gold. The ancient Egyptians, building on Aristotle's teachings, believed it should be possible to hurry up the process. The Egyptians invented alchemy, the would-be science of turning base metals into gold, which attracted generations of adherents all over the world.

Iron seemed like a likely candidate to be turned into gold. First, it seemed eager to change: It turned so easily to rust. When mixed with other substances, it transformed readily. However, much to the alchemists' disappointment, they were never able to transform iron——or any other substance——into gold.

CHAPTER THREE
The Science of Iron

DISPROVING THE ANCIENT GREEKS

In the fifth century B.C., the Greek philosopher Empedocles proposed that all matter is made up of a combination of four elements: earth, fire, air, and water. His idea became well accepted in the ancient Greek world. Iron, which inevitably rusted over time, seemed to provide vivid proof of this theory. The ancient Greeks believed that iron rusted because the elements of water, air, and fire eventually left iron, leaving only the red earth (rust) behind.

Empedocles's and his fellow philosophers' ideas about matter were accepted for about two thousand years. Then, in the 1770s, a French scientist named Antoine Lavoisier challenged the ancient Greeks. He conducted an experiment with iron filings (tiny pieces of iron) and water. First, he weighed the unrusted iron and then submerged it in water until it rusted. Then he removed the rust-covered iron, carefully dried it, and reweighed it. He discovered that the rusty iron filings weighed *more* than the unrusted iron filings. The water had taken nothing from the iron. In fact, the dried, rusted iron filings weighed

This illustration of Antoine Laurent de Lavoisier in his laboratory is from a nineteenth-century book by E. Mennechet.

more than they did before they rusted, so something had been added to them!

What had happened? Water—as Lavoisier suspected—is a compound (a substance made of two or more elements chemically bonded) of two gases. One gas he named oxygen; the other would become known as hydrogen. The oxygen from the water combined with the iron to form a new compound—*rust*—while a little hydrogen was liberated from the water. The rusted iron filings weighed more because oxygen had been added to them.

Lavoisier's experiment proved the ancient Greeks wrong about two of their elements. The rust that they called earth was not an element at all because it was made of iron and oxygen. Water was not an element either because it, too, was composed of more than one substance.

Until the eighteenth century, scientists didn't conduct experiments. They made observations, thought about what could account for those observations, and then formed a theory that accounted for what they had observed. The ancient Greek philosophers, for example, observed that when a green stick burned, fire, smoke (air), and steam (water) rose from the stick. All that remained was ash, which the ancient Greeks believed to be gray earth. This and other observations led them to conclude that all matter in the world was made up of different proportions of four indivisible elements: earth, air, water, and fire.

Lavoisier was one of the first scientists who used a different method, the scientific method, to understand the natural world. He made a hypothesis (a possible explanation for a set of observations), proposed an experiment and made predictions about its outcome, tested the predictions through experimentation, and repeated the experiment to make sure the results were always the same.

IRON, AN ELEMENT

Lavoisier and other chemists soon identified a number of substances including iron that—unlike earth, air, water, and fire—were elements in the modern sense of the word. An element is defined by modern chemists as a substance made of atoms of only one kind that cannot be broken down by chemical means. Scientists have identified more than one hundred elements.

At the center (called the nucleus) of any atom is a cluster of particles called protons. The protons have a positive (+) electrical charge. Mixed in with the protons are neutrons, particles that are similar in size to protons but have no electrical charge. Whizzing around the nucleus are electrons, which have a negative (–) charge. (Particles with opposite charges attract each other. That's why electrons don't whiz off into space: They are attracted by the positively charged protons.) The number of electrons in an electrically neutral atom is identical to the number of its protons.

Antoine Laurent Lavoisier was one of the world's greatest scientists. He earned the money to do his research in chemistry by working as a tax collector and in other positions for the government of King Louis XVI. When the French overthrew the monarchy in 1789, Lavoisier, despite his international fame, became suspect. Not only had he worked for the king, but he had antagonized a man named Jean-Paul Marat who became one of the French Revolution's leaders. (Marat, a scientist before the Revolution, had applied for membership to the French Academy of Sciences. Lavoisier had opposed him on the grounds that he was a poor chemist.) Unfortunately for Lavoisier—and for the progress of science—Lavoisier's troubles with Marat and his association with the king led to his beheading in 1794.

Atomic particles—protons, neutrons, and electrons—are identical no matter what element they are in. What makes an iron atom different from a gold atom is the number of protons and neutrons in its nucleus. Gold, for example, has 79 protons (and 79 electrons) and usually 118 neutrons. Iron has 26 protons (and 26 electrons) and usually 30 neutrons.

The 26 electrons circling the nucleus of an iron atom are arranged in a way that enables two or three of its electrons to be easily shared with atoms of oxygen and certain other elements. When an oxygen atom and an iron atom share these electrons, the two atoms are chemically bonded.

PURIFYING IRON

About 90 percent of the molten core of Earth is made of iron. Unfortunately, the iron in the core is far too deep to mine. Five percent of the Earth's crust (the surface layer) is also made of iron, but the iron is difficult to remove because it is almost always bonded with oxygen or other elements. It takes great heat and a chemical reaction to break those bonds to get pure iron.

How does heating separate the iron from the oxygen? Most furnaces burn charcoal or gas, both of which contain carbon. As these fuels burn, they release hot carbon. Hot carbon has a strong affinity for

In chemistry, the symbol for iron is Fe, which comes from the Latin word for iron, *ferrum*. Much of the iron ore from which manufacturers extract pure iron contains the compound ferric oxide, which is also called iron oxide. In ferric oxide, two atoms of iron are bonded with three atoms of oxygen. The symbol for ferric oxide is Fe_2O_3.

(chemical attraction to) oxygen. The hot carbon strips away the oxygen from the iron to form compounds called carbon monoxide (CO) and carbon dioxide in (CO_2). In carbon monoxide, one atom of carbon is bonded with one atom of oxygen. In carbon dioxide, one atom of carbon is bonded with two atoms of oxygen. In both cases, pure iron is left.

HARDENING IRON

As we saw in Chapter One, ancient Near Eastern blacksmiths discovered that heating iron directly on charcoal under certain conditions made it harder. Why? Iron atoms, as well as the atoms of other metals, stick closely together as crystals. (A crystal is any substance with an orderly three-dimensional arrangement of atoms or molecules.)

To envision what an iron crystal is like, think of a box with several layers of marbles, one on top of the other. The marbles represent atoms in a crystal of iron.

A crystal of iron is also called a grain of iron. In a piece of iron, grains of different sizes and shapes are closely packed together. When iron is heated in a charcoal furnace, carbon atoms are able to squeeze into some of the spaces between the atoms in the grains. Carbon atoms also squeeze into some of the spaces between grains. The carbon acts like cement in the iron crystal, and the layers of iron and the grains of iron no longer slip so easily past each other. The iron has been converted to a harder substance—a kind of steel. Steel is iron treated with intense heat and mixed with carbon to make it hard and tough.

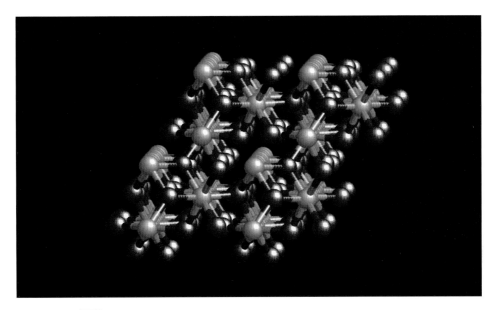

This is one possible crystal form a metal can take. There are many others.

The ancient blacksmiths also found that repeatedly hammering and reheating iron strengthened it. We now know that when blacksmiths hammer the surface of iron, they break some of the crystal structure, compressing some grains so they are packed more densely. The hammering also reduces the size of the grains, which increases the strength of the metal.

The temperature of the iron is critical in determining how much carbon gets into the iron. Getting just the right amount of carbon (so that carbon is about 1 percent of the total mass of the metal) into iron was very tricky for all the early blacksmiths, who had no way to precisely measure temperature.

Ancient blacksmiths in the West had trouble making their furnaces hot enough to allow carbon into their iron. Ancient Chinese blacksmiths managed, with their sophisticated bellows, to make furnaces hot enough to melt iron. But in their hot furnaces, too much carbon (about 3.5 percent) entered the iron. Their cast iron was brittle and couldn't be shaped further after it was formed.

As you will see, the story of iron in the modern era is the story of getting just the right amount of carbon into iron to make steel.

CHAPTER FOUR
A Revolution in Iron and Steel

THE FIERY FURNACE

After the fall of the Roman Empire in about A.D. 500, Europeans made little progress in iron making. They continued to heat and hammer bloom iron to make a wrought-iron object, and then, by heating the wrought iron directly on charcoal, they turned the outer layer of the object to steel. This "bloomery process" was slow, and blacksmiths had to make iron objects one at a time.

Europeans recognized that forcing air into the furnace would make it burn hotter, but it was not until the fourteenth century that they figured out a way to do this efficiently. Millers (people who grind grain into flour) had been using waterwheels constructed over fast-flowing streams to power huge grindstones for a long time. Around 1300, someone in Europe connected a pair of bellows to a waterwheel. As the water turned the wheel, the wheel pumped one bellows and then the second bellows so that a continuous stream of air was blasted through a hole called a tuyere into the furnace.

These *blast furnaces*, as they were called in Europe, raised the temperature inside the furnace to about 2102°F (1150°C), the temperature at which the iron suddenly absorbs as much carbon as it can, about 4 percent. That much carbon incorporated into the iron lowers the melting point of the iron, and molten iron—ready to be cast—flows out of the furnace. By 1400 there were blast furnaces across northern Europe and great demand for cast-iron objects. Cast-iron objects required much less labor and were cheaper to produce than ones of hammered wrought iron.

It took huge bellows like these to blast air into a medieval blast furnace.

The stone furnaces designed by the Romans were squat. During the 1300s, furnaces were redesigned. They became taller until they were more than three stories tall and 10 feet (3 meters) wide. The new shape produced higher temperatures and allowed more iron ore to be smelted at one time.

To make cast iron, the iron maker first had to heat the furnace to a working temperature. Then he fed a mixture of charcoal, limestone, and iron ore in the top of the furnace. As the charcoal burned and melted the iron, more raw materials were added to the top. Air was blasted in via the tuyere near the bottom of the furnace. Molten material—liquid iron with the lighter, melted slag floating on top—ran out of the bottom on the side opposite the tuyere. The molten slag was siphoned off and the iron allowed to run into molds to cool and harden.

The iron that came out of the blast furnaces was called *pig iron*. That's because the iron ran out into a trench dug in the ground and then into several large, shallow depressions that stuck out at right angles to the trench. Someone thought that the arrangement looked like a sow suckling her pigs: hence, pig iron!

FUEL FOR THE FIERY FURNACE

The growth of iron making radically changed the look of Europe and especially of England. Not only did noisy, smoky blast furnaces, which operated night and day, dot the countryside but iron making transformed the natural landscape itself. Iron-making furnaces required huge amounts of fuel. That fuel was charcoal, and charcoal was made from wood. For

Charcoal—like the charcoal we use in backyard grills—is wood that is slowly and partially burned under cover so that water and other volatile (easily burned) elements are eliminated. What is left is nearly pure carbon, which burns very hot and with little smoke. Charcoal was the essential fuel for blast furnaces.

■ ■ ■

Coal is a naturally occurring black substance made from layers of partly decayed plant matter that has been squeezed and hardened underground. It took millions of years for the coal we use today to be formed. Coke was made by making a big pile of coal around a small brick chimney and covering it with earth so only a little air could get in. The coal pile was lit and allowed to smolder for many hours until all the coal had been "coked."

every pound of iron produced, 5 pounds (2 kilograms) of charcoal, which was made from 15 to 20 pounds (7 to 9 kilograms) of wood, went into the furnace.

In ancient Roman times, the need for charcoal led to the complete destruction of all the trees on Cyprus, an island in the eastern Mediterranean. In the late Middle Ages, huge tracts of European forest fell to the axe to make charcoal for the iron-making furnaces. By 1600, England was facing an energy crisis. The great oak and beech forests that once blanketed the land were largely gone; England had become a landscape of rolling green—but treeless—fields. There simply weren't enough trees to supply all the charcoal needed for the blast furnaces. England's production of iron began to fall.

The answer to the crisis was coal. In England, people had known about coal for centuries, and as the forests vanished and charcoal became more expensive, they increasingly turned to coal to heat their homes. Some industries, such as glassmaking, had adapted to coal. But coal didn't work for iron making. Iron makers had always mixed charcoal and iron ore together in the

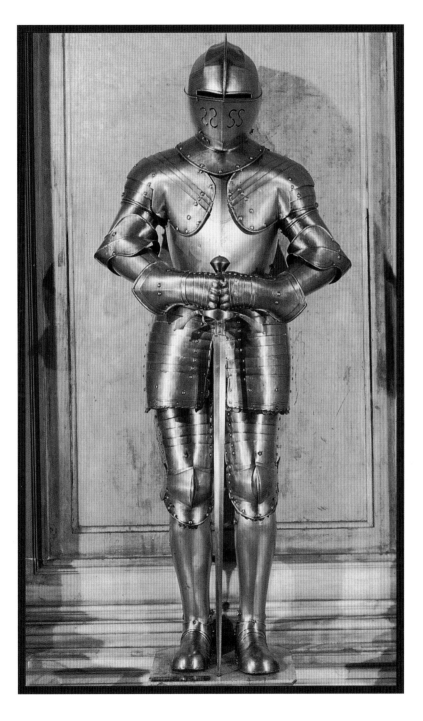

Knights in the early Middle Ages wore chain mail armor. By the 1300s knights wore plate armor as protection from arrows fired from long bows or crossbows that could pierce chain mail. This armor consisted of large pieces of steel. A knight's helmet, too, was made of pieces of steel. The cost, it is estimated, of equipping a knight and his horse in armor was equivalent to the cost of an army tank today!

furnace. When they tried this method with coal, the iron they produced was brittle because the other elements in coal—chiefly phosphorus and sulfur—contaminated the iron.

Then in 1707 an Englishman named Abraham Darby came up with a solution. Darby had decided to manufacture thin-walled cooking pots from cast iron. He knew that breweries used coke, a fuel made from partially burned coal, to heat the ovens that dried malt, one of beer's ingredients. Brewers had found that beer tasted awful when the malt was heated in coal-burning ovens, but when they burned coke instead, the problem was solved. Darby wondered if the impurities in coal that gave beer a bad taste were also responsible for making coal-smelted iron brittle.

Darby was right. In 1709 he began producing high-quality cast iron using a coke-burning furnace. England is very rich in coal, and before long, most of the blast furnaces in England were burning coke. The demand for coal for blast furnaces drew thousands of former farmworkers into coal mining. The iron-making industry expanded, too, and blast furnaces and foundries (places where pig iron is worked into objects) spread across England. For the next 250 years, British iron dominated the world.

IRON AND THE INDUSTRIAL REVOLUTION

The Industrial Revolution began in England in the mid-1700s and then spread to northern Europe and America in the early 1800s. It had many causes, and technological innovation was one of them. The "water frame," a machine patented by Richard Arkwright in 1769, spun dozens of threads of strong cotton simultaneously. The water frame and the "cotton gin" ("gin" was another word for engine), invented by the American Eli Whitney in 1793 to separate cotton fibers from cotton seeds, speeded up production of cotton cloth immensely. These two machines changed textile production from a home-based occupation to a factory-based industry.

The steam engine was another technological innovation that drove the Industrial Revolution. English inventor Thomas Savesy had invented a steam-driven pump in 1698, but it was too inefficient to be of much use. After James Watt improved the design in 1769, the steam engine began to change English manufacturing dramatically. Watt's engines provided cheap, continuous power to pump water out of coal mines and run the machines that produced textiles and other manufactures.

The steam engines were made of iron, and so were many other innovations of the Industrial Revolution. The textile looms had iron parts. The railroads used iron locomotives and iron rails. Trains crossed bridges made of cast-iron trusses. (The grandson of Abraham Darby cast the iron trusses for the world's first iron bridge in 1780.) In 1843 the S.S. *Great Britain*, the world's first iron-hulled ship, steamed off from the dock at Bristol. In 1889 the Eiffel Tower, made of iron lattice, was completed. Thanks to blast-furnace technology, iron became an everyday material, much like plastic is today. People ate with iron forks, knives, and spoons, cooked in iron pots, and opened doors with iron hinges. Wagons rolled on iron wheels, and farmers used iron rakes, hoes, spades, and other tools.

All the iron in the wheels, hoes, bridges, rails, and steam engines was cast iron. But remember the drawbacks to cast

iron? It couldn't be worked in any way after it had been cast and cooled in a mold. A piece of cast iron was brittle, too, unless it was roasted with charcoal in a closed furnace. Even so, the iron was not nearly so strong as if it had been steel all the way through.

IMPROVEMENTS IN STEELMAKING

In the 1740s an English clockmaker named Benjamin Huntsman invented a version of the ancient Indian method for making steel. Huntsman, who needed stronger steel springs for his clocks, burned charcoal and wrought iron in a closed crucible. The result was a metal that was steel all the way through. About the same time, English iron makers, like the ancient Chinese before them, discovered that when they stirred molten iron, they combined oxygen from the air with the carbon in the iron. Stirring reduced the carbon content of the iron, turning it into steel. But steel makers using crucibles or stirring molten iron could only make small quantities of steel at one time.

Then in 1855 an English engineer named Henry Bessemer took a different approach. He redesigned the blast furnace, blasting air into the molten iron through pipes from below. Most people thought he was crazy: Surely the air would cool the molten iron and solidify it in the furnace, they thought. But when he tried it, the results were just the opposite: A shower of burning gases, sparks, and smoke shot out of the top of the furnace . . . and molten steel ran out the bottom!

Adding that much oxygen so quickly created an exothermic (heat-producing) chemical reaction between the carbon and the oxygen, which allowed the carbon to be rapidly burned out of the molten iron.

The furnaces in England and elsewhere worked around the clock, lighting up the night sky with a red glare and roaring like thunder as air blasted through them. Adult ironworkers, despite their hard labor, weren't paid enough money to support a family, so their children had to work, too. A British government report on the conditions in the metal manufacturing industry in 1840 gives chilling details of children's lives. Girls and boys went to work at the age of eight or even younger and often worked fifteen or sixteen hours a day. The work was noisy and dangerous, and the workrooms could be suffocatingly hot or numbingly cold. Children frequently were burned by sparks flying off the hot iron.

William Kelly, an American, also invented a process to make mild steel about the same time Bessemer did. The son of Irish immigrants, he started a business making iron pots in Kentucky. One day while he was trying to hurry the cooling of a bucket of molten iron, he blew cool air on it with a bellow. Fumes blew off from the bucket, making him pass out.

When Kelly thought about the incident, it occurred to him that oxygen in the air had combined with carbon in the molten iron to create poisonous carbon monoxide. To test his idea, he built a furnace that would blow air on hot iron to see if he could remove carbon from molten iron. (This time, he vented the fumes!) His process worked. But by the time he was able to convince people of his success, Bessemer had already patented a more sophisticated process. Although the method is named for Bessemer, Kelly may have developed it first.

What Bessemer produced was *mild steel*, which is cast iron with just enough carbon so that it can be worked after it is poured. Knives made of mild steel can be ground to sharpness. Mild steel bars can be reheated and bent, twisted, pulled and rolled into flat sheets.

Bessemer's steel was no more expensive to produce than cast iron because the only additional ingredient was air. With Bessemer's process, steelmakers could adjust the quality of steel they produced to suit their needs. For example, by reducing the length of time that air was piped into the molten iron, more carbon could be retained, making the steel harder but less flexible.

Cheap, strong, tough steel that could be produced in large quantities changed forever the way people around the world live. Steel was essential to making engines for airplanes and other vehicles, cheaper rails for railroads, reinforced concrete for highways, and the internal structures of skyscrapers. Although English entrepreneurs had dominated the steel industry for two hundred years, it would be Americans who pushed forward to new frontiers in steel manufacture.

46

Steel is lighter and stronger than iron. If the Eiffel Tower were rebuilt today using steel instead of iron, the builders would need only one-third the amount of steel.

Replica of the first steel plow
built by John Deere in 1837

McCormick's
Reaper, illustrated
here by Burgess
and Key, was first
patented in 1834.

Modern farm machinery

CHAPTER FIVE
New Frontiers in Steel

STEEL ON THE FARM

As pioneer farmers settled land west of the Mississippi River in the nineteenth century, they discovered that the soil in the Midwest was very difficult to plow with the iron plows of the day. Their plows were designed for the light, sandy soil of New England, which easily slipped off the plow blade. The rich, thick, fertile soil of the Midwest clung to the plow. Farmers had to stop every few steps to scrape off the dirt. It made plowing slow and discouraging work.

John Deere was a Vermont native who grew up to be a blacksmith in the town of Middlebury, Vermont. In the mid-1830s an economic depression hit Vermont. Deere, like many other young Vermonters of the time, decided to try his luck out West. Leaving his wife and children behind temporarily, he traveled by canal boat and stagecoach and ended up in the village of Grand Detour, Illinois. Within two days of his arrival, he had built a forge and started work.

Deere was intrigued with the problem of plowing the tough midwestern sod. He began experimenting with a new plow design and soon had fashioned one from a broken steel saw. His plow had a highly polished surface and a steeply sloped shape. The thick midwestern soil peeled neatly off the plow. Deere began to manufacture plows and quickly discovered that getting enough steel was a problem. He made his first plows with discarded steel, but then had to order steel from England at great expense. In 1846 he received his first shipment of steel from Pittsburgh, Pennsylvania, a city that was becoming the steelmaking center of America. During the next year, he made a thousand steel plows.

The large size of American farms and the short supply of laborers inspired other innovations in farm machinery. In the mid-1800s, Cyrus McCormick invented harvesters that reaped and bound wheat, hay mowers, and other agricultural machines—knives, wheels, reels, and frames made of mild steel. Vast acres of western prairies became farmland with the help of steel. In the 1870s almost 200 million acres (80 million hectares) of midwestern land—an area equal to the size of Great Britain and France combined—were converted to farmland.

Barbed steel wire, which was made of two long strands of wire twisted together with small, sharp wire pieces twisted between them at short intervals, was another innovation that changed the American West. Before barbed wire was invented, fencing the vast acres where cattle grazed out West was prohibitively expensive and required a lot of effort. After Joseph Glidden patented a machine to manufacture barbed wire in 1874, ranchers and farmers were able to fence their land quickly and cheaply. By 1890 most of the American West was fenced. This meant, however, that "free range grazers" (cattle

Andrew Carnegie, born in a small stone cottage in Scotland in 1835, became one of America's first steelmaking tycoons. Andrew's father, a weaver, worked on a hand loom. When power looms run by steam engines replaced hand looms, he lost his job. Unable to find other work, he decided to emigrate with his family to America.

At the age of thirteen, Andrew got a job in a textile factory in Allegheny, Pennsylvania, working twelve-hour days. Next he became a messenger boy for a telegraph company, then an assistant in a railroad company, and eventually an executive of the railroad company. He saved most of what he earned and invested it in the booming businesses of the day—railroads and oil—and made a fortune by the time he was thirty-three. In 1883 he bought the Pittsburgh Bessemer Steel Company in Homestead, Pennsylvania. Carnegie bought at just the right time. There was a huge demand in America for steel.

Carnegie's company, which he renamed Homestead Steel Works, was very successful. But Carnegie was not the only Pennsylvania steel producer of the time. Because Pittsburgh is close to coal mines and river transportation, it attracted other steel mills. By the end of the century, Pittsburgh steel companies produced more steel than all of Europe combined.

Carnegie was one of many Americans who became very wealthy as a result of the boom in steel and related railroad enterprises. J. P. Morgan ran another steel giant, U.S. Steel Corporation. Edward Henry Harriman owned and invested in railroads, which made him a huge fortune. Henry Clay Frick, another American industrial magnate, was involved in both the steel and the railroad business.

owners who grazed their herds freely without regard to the ownership of land) lost their livelihoods. It also meant that ranchers became dependent on the railroads to move their cattle to market because the fences prevented them from driving cattle across the prairie to Kansas City and other cattle markets.

STEEL AND THE RAILROADS

In the second half of the 1800s, Americans were settling the far reaches of the country and discovering its vast natural resources. They found gold in California; copper, silver, and iron ore in the upper Midwest; and coal in Pennsylvania and West Virginia.

Mine owners and farmers needed to get their goods to markets. Railroads were the best way to cover the vast distances between mines and farmland and cities. Yet at the end of the Civil War in 1865, there were only 35,000 miles (56,000 kilometers) of railway in the United States, most of it running through the northern states. It was impossible to go from the East Coast to the West Coast by rail. But that changed in 1869 when the Union Pacific railroad company, laying rails from east to west, and the Central Pacific railroad company, laying rails from west to east, met in Utah. A transcontinental railroad was born. At the same time workers ran a telegraph line alongside the rails. Now information could pass quickly between the coasts. By the end of the century, there were 200,000 miles (322,000 kilometers) of rail crisscrossing the country.

SKYSCRAPERS

Railroads needed vast amounts of steel, but so did skyscrapers. By the late 1800s, people were flooding into American cities, especially New York and Chicago, attracted by the new industrial and office jobs there. They needed more space to work and live in. Architects looked for a way to build up, not just out.

In buildings made with brick or stone, builders have to add strength to the bottom floors as more floors are added on top. This means the walls of the lower floors become thicker and thicker as the building grows higher. It made no sense to design a brick or stone building more than about fifteen stories tall because the walls of the lower floors had to be so thick that there was little living or working space left.

Bessemer steel made skyscrapers possible. Builders could construct a skeleton of horizontal steel girder beams welded to vertical steel columns. In this design, all the weight of the floors is transferred down through the columns into the base of the building. At the base are cast-iron plates that sit on top of stacks of steel beams that rest on poured concrete pads.

The outer walls of a skyscraper are called curtain walls. That's because they simply separate the outdoor elements from the office or living space inside, like a curtain. Skyscrapers' curtain walls support their own weight, not the weight of the building. The real support for the building is its steel-beam skeleton.

The ten-story Home Insurance Building in Chicago built in 1885 is considered the first skyscraper. Skyscrapers were an American invention, but today skyscrapers are common throughout the world. In the modern skyscraper at right you can clearly see that the exterior walls are curtain walls!

OTHER USES OF STEEL

The early twentieth century could be called the Steel Age. Steel made all kinds of new inventions and technologies possible. Elevators used steel cables to support the weight of the cab. Automobiles, which used lots of steel in their bodies and motors, became a common sight on city streets in the first decades of the twentieth century. By 1915 more than a million Ford Model Ts alone had been manufactured. Steel made bridges like the Brooklyn Bridge, which spans the East River to Manhattan in New York, feasible. The Brooklyn Bridge, completed in 1883, was the first steel cable suspension bridge.

Ships were made of steel. Submarines, which became a part of several countries' naval forces in the early 1900s, would have been impossible without steel. Most early airplanes were made primarily of wood and fabric, although by World War I and the 1920s, many had tubular-steel fuselage frameworks. By the early 1930s, it was possible to mass-produce all-metal airplanes, and all-metal airplanes (made of steel alloys as well as aluminum) became the norm.

Steel, often alloyed with other metals, became a part of everyday life. Steel was cheap, tough, and long lasting. It could be poured into almost any shape, as well as rolled flat and pulled into wires. Millions of miles of steel pipe were laid underground to carry water, oil, and gas to consumers. There was steel in road signs, street lamps, refrigerators and other household appliance housings, food cans, cutlery and kitchen knives, scissors, nail clippers, tweezers, zippers, nails, and hundreds of other common objects.

A marvel of engineering—the Brooklyn Bridge as seen from its pedestrian walkway. The bridge deck is supported by four steel cables, each about 16 inches (40 cm) in diameter. The cables contain 5,434 wires, for a total length of about 14,000 miles (22,400 kilometers) of steel wire. That's more than enough wire to stretch from the North Pole to the South Pole!

IRON, MAGNETS, AND MOTORS

Iron and steel have revolutionized our lives in another way. In ancient China, Greece, and elsewhere, people discovered that a certain kind of stone had peculiar abilities. In the fourth century B.C. in China, magicians noticed that a spoon made out of the stone always turned on its bowl and pointed north. The Chinese called it *tzu shih*, the "loving stone," because it attracted bits of iron to it. They used the stone spoon balanced on a plate as a compass. By about A.D. 650, the Chinese learned that if they rubbed an iron needle against the stone, it, too, pointed north.

The stone they used was a piece of lodestone, a variety of magnetite that is naturally magnetic. One end of a piece of lodestone, or a piece of iron or steel that has been magnetized, points north and the other points south. It does this because our Earth has a core of molten iron that acts, in essence, as a giant magnet. The ends of magnetized stones, bars, and needles are attracted to the north and south ends of the Earth.

In 1000 someone discovered that when steel was poured into a mold that was aligned in a north-south direction and quickly cooled, the steel would become permanently magnetized. Lodestone was no longer necessary.

The invention of marine compasses (in China about 850 and in Europe and the Middle East about 1200) revolutionized travel and allowed explorers to find new lands. With needles magnetized by lodestone, sailors could leave the sight of shore and find their way on open water where there are no landmarks. They could sail in the right direction even when they couldn't see the Sun or the North Star.

The magnetic quality of iron inspired perhaps a greater invention in the beginning of the nineteenth century. In 1820, Danish scientist Hans Oersted was conducting a demonstration of how electricity flowed from a battery through a wire. In the midst of his demonstration, he noticed that the needle of a compass lying nearby moved whenever electricity flowed through the wire. Oersted experimented and found that he was generating a cylindrical magnetic field around the wire. The electrified wire created a magnetic field that influenced the compass needle.

In 1825, English experimenter William Sturgeon found that when he wound coils of wire around a piece of iron and sent electricity through the wire, he increased the magnetic force of the iron dramatically. His device, an *electromagnet*, could lift many times its own weight.

Michael Faraday was an apprentice scientist in England at this time, and he was fascinated by Oersted's and Sturgeon's results. He wondered: If electricity could generate magnetism, didn't it make sense that magnetism could generate electricity? Faraday worked for years to solve this question. He tried all sorts of arrangements of copper wire and iron *magnets* to see if he could produce electricity. Finally, after ten years of effort, he did. He found that when he made a coil of the copper wire and dipped the magnet in and out of the coil, he generated

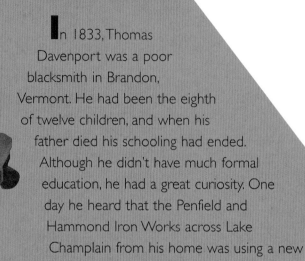

In 1833, Thomas Davenport was a poor blacksmith in Brandon, Vermont. He had been the eighth of twelve children, and when his father died his schooling had ended. Although he didn't have much formal education, he had a great curiosity. One day he heard that the Penfield and Hammond Iron Works across Lake Champlain from his home was using a new invention called an electromagnet to separate iron ore from useless rock. As a blacksmith, Davenport was intrigued and went to see it. What he saw was a barrel with iron spikes that had been magnetized with an electromagnet. The barrel turned and the magnetized spikes attracted the highest-quality iron out of the crushed rock that passed beneath.

Davenport wondered if it would be possible to produce mechanical motion—work—from an electromagnet. He bought a large electromagnet, took it apart to see how it worked, and then built two of his own, as well as a chemical battery. He attached one electromagnet to a wheel and the other to a frame. The two magnets attracted each other and caused the wheel to turn half a revolution. Then, by reversing the wires to one of the magnets, he reversed the magnet's poles, and got the wheel to complete the turn.

Davenport then invented a device that automatically switched the poles. In 1837 he received the first patent for an electric motor. However, only when electric power became available by wire from large generators in the 1880s did electric motors come into their own.

electricity. Moving the magnet—interrupting the magnetic field—was the key to success.

Electromagnets, generators, and motors changed the industrial world, as well as the lives of individuals. When these inventions were coupled with the strong, cheap steel produced by the Bessemer process, our modern world had arrived.

Molten iron pours into a massive bucket at this modern German steelmill.

CHAPTER SIX
Steel Today

MODERN STEELMAKING

In the year 2000, nearly 846 million tons (770 million metric tons) of raw steel were produced around the world. Ninety-three percent of all global metal production was steel! Most of that steel was made in one of two modern processes.

The basic oxygen process is a modification of the nineteenth-century Bessemer process. Today, molten iron and scrap steel is mixed in a furnace that looks like a giant concrete mixer. The furnace is tipped to one side when the ingredients are poured in the top of the mixer. When it is returned to its upright position, a tube is pushed down inside. The tube delivers a blast of pure oxygen, which makes the iron and steel burn quickly and hot.

After the temperature and quality of the molten steel have been checked, the furnace is tipped so that the molten steel can be poured out. The impurities that remain from the molten iron have turned to slag and are left at the bottom of the furnace. After the steel has been poured, the furnace is turned upside down to remove the slag.

Unlike the basic oxygen process, the electric arc process does not start with molten metal. The electric arc furnace is filled with recycled goods made from steel, such as cars and washing machines that have reached the end of their useful life or the steel debris from demolished buildings. Sometimes pig iron is added, too.

An overhead crane tips the cold steel and iron into the furnace. A lid swings onto the top of the furnace. The lid contains electrodes that go into the furnace. When electricity flows through the electrodes, they form an arc of electrical current, which melts the metal. It takes a lot of electricity to create the arc—enough to power a small city!

As the iron and steel melt, other metals are added to make alloys. Then the furnace is tilted to one side so that the slag floating on the surface of the molten steel can be poured off. Finally, the furnace is tipped to the other side and the liquid steel is poured out. The modern electric arc furnace can make 150 tons (136 metric tons) of steel in about ninety minutes.

STEEL AND THE ENVIRONMENT

It has always taken an enormous amount of energy to separate iron from iron ore and to heat steel to the high temperatures needed to make it liquefy. We saw how, before coke replaced charcoal as a fuel, the forests of England and other European countries were denuded by the demand for fuel for the iron and steel furnaces. Steelmaking also produces a lot of smoke, metal dust, and other airborne pollution.

Pittsburgh, which became known as "Smoky City" as well as "Steel City" in the late nineteenth and twentieth centuries, was once the dirtiest, most polluted city in America. The coke-making ovens and steel factories produced so much smoke that sometimes streetlights and car headlights had to be turned on during the day. People who worked in downtown offices sometimes had to change their shirts during the day because they had become gray with soot.

In the 1940s and 1950s, the municipal government of Pittsburgh decided to clean up the city. It enacted pollution controls that forced steel mills to partially clean the smoke before releasing it into the air. Federal legislation, enforced by the U.S. Environmental Protection Agency founded in 1970, brought even stricter air-pollution controls in the following decades, both to steel mills in Pittsburgh and to other industrial operations in the United States. Today, the North American steel industry directs about 15 percent of the money it invests in new buildings and equipment to pollution control equipment. The U.S. industry has reduced the amount of energy needed to produce a ton of steel by almost 50 percent in the last twenty-five years and reduced its discharge of air and water pollution by 90 percent. Many old, polluting, and inefficient plants have been closed, and the new mills are better designed to minimize polluting emissions.

Despite its negative impact, steel does have significant environmental benefits: It can be endlessly recycled without ever losing its quality. About half the steel produced in 2000 was made from recycled steel. Each year, steel recycling saves enough energy to provide power to 18 million households. Moreover, as steel technology improves, engineers are able to make steel stronger and stronger per pound, so those manufacturers that use steel in their products need less of it.

MODERN USAGE AND NEW STEEL

Steel continues to be a part of our lives. From its birth in the early twentieth century, the automobile industry has used huge amounts of steel. North American automakers and their parts suppliers used about 18 million tons (16 million metric tons) of steel in their vehicles in 1998 alone. The average vehicle contained about 1,810 pounds (822 kilograms) of flat-rolled, bar, tubular, rod, and wire steel. In addition, there is steel in the roads those vehicles travel. In the United States, there are 2.3 million miles (3.7 million kilometers) of concrete roadway that is strengthened by steel rods.

In most homes today a lumber frame supports the roof, floors, and walls. But a growing number of homes are being built with lightweight steel frames. Steel is more expensive than wood, but it doesn't warp and termites don't eat it.

You will find steel everywhere in your house, including in your watch, pots and pans, picture frames, file cabinets, bottle caps, trophies, toys, wastebaskets, and even the kitchen sink! Each year about 4.5 million tons (4 million metric tons) of steel go into home and office equipment and appliances, such as refrigerators, microwaves, air conditioners, washers and dryers, toasters, grills, and kitchen ranges. (Designers are now working on polymer coatings for steel containers so that they can go safely into a microwave.) More than 37 billion steel food cans come off the production line each year in the United States and Canada. Some people also have steel in their bod-

Stainless steel flatware

Stainless steel teakettle

Stainless steel skate blades

ies. Pins that hold broken bones together are made of steel and so are some artificial hips.

Many modern products use steel alloys. Steel alloys are made of steel plus such metals as chromium, tungsten, nickel, and cobalt. *Stainless steel* is steel that has at least 10.5 percent chromium. The chromium reacts chemically with air to form a protective coating on the steel that prevents the iron in the steel from combining with air and rusting. Often, nickel and molybdenum are also added to stainless steel for corrosion protection and for strength.

Sometimes, steel is coated with another material to prevent rust. Steel food cans are coated with tin and steel; electricity pylons (towers) are coated with plastic. Steel that is exposed to weather, such as the steel in automobiles, silos, and metal roofs, gets a coat of zinc or a zinc/aluminum alloy to prevent rust.

High-speed drill bits often contain the metal cobalt. A steel/cobalt alloy remains hard even when red hot. Knife manufacturers work with steel/tungsten alloys because tungsten strengthens the steel and makes it resistant to wear.

In modern steel mills, the amount of carbon and other metals added to steel can be precisely controlled for the right combination of strength, weight, and flexibility to fit a user's needs. Steel engineers continue to develop new, thinner, and stronger steels. The solid rocket boosters, for example, that carry the space shuttle into orbit are made of steel segments joined with special high-strength steel-alloy pins. With today's technology, steel alloys can be custom-designed for almost any use or condition. The future looks bright for steel!

Airplane landing gear like this is made of steel alloyed with a little chromium and a little vanadium. Landing gear springs made of this alloy can be folded and flattened without breaking.

SCOTLAND

SCANDINAVIA

GREAT BRITAIN

HOLLAND

IRELAND

ENGLAND
WALES
London

GERMANY

RUS

EUROPE

ATLANTIC

Paris

GAUL
FRANCE

ALPS

Danube R.

OCEAN

ITALY

Rome

BLACK SEA

CAUCASUS

THRACE

Constantinople (Istanbul)

PORTUGAL

Iberian Peninsula

PHRYGIA

Hattusa

MEDITERRANEAN SEA

GREECE

TURKEY

ASSYRIA

Nineveh

ATLAS MTNS.

Athens

Cyprus

SUMERIA

Calah

Tigris R.

SYRIA

MESOPOTAMIA

Euphrates R.

PHOENICIA

BABYLONIA

Alexandria

Jerusalem

SAHARA DESERT

Memphis
(Cairo)

Jericho

ARABIA

EGYPT

ARABIAN
DESERT

RED SEA

Nile R.

Mecca

AFRICA

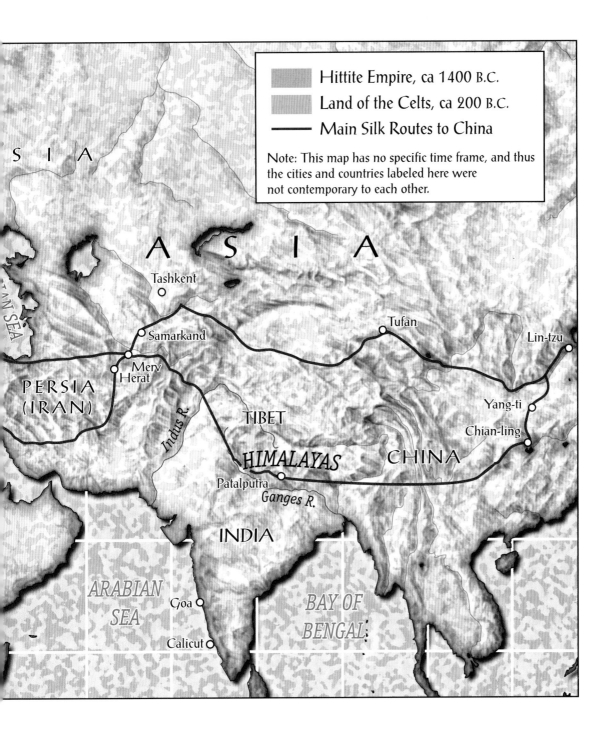

Hittite Empire, ca 1400 B.C.

Land of the Celts, ca 200 B.C.

Main Silk Routes to China

Note: This map has no specific time frame, and thus
the cities and countries labeled here were
not contemporary to each other.

ASIA

A S I A

Tashkent

Tufan

Lin-tzu

Samarkand

Yang-ti

Merv
Herat

Chian-ling

PERSIA
(IRAN)

TIBET

CHINA

Indus R.

HIMALAYAS

Patalputra

Ganges R.

INDIA

ARABIAN
SEA

Goa

BAY OF
BENGAL

Calicut

Timeline

B.C.

1400s People in Near East begin smelting iron; Hittites discover how to make wrought iron and iron with a carburized (steel) surface

1200 Hittite empire collapses and iron-making technology spreads throughout Near East

1000 Beginning of Iron Age in the Near East; iron replaces bronze as the most popular metal for making tools and weapons

700 Iron-making technology spreads into Europe

650 Chinese make wrought iron

500s Celts invent chain mail made of iron rings; Chinese invent cast iron

500 Indians begin making wootz steel

300s Romans learn to make tempered steel

A.D. 850   Chinese invent the marine compass with a magnetized iron needle

1300   Europeans make cast iron using blast furnaces

1600s   English begin using coal to produce iron and steel

1709   First high-quality cast iron made in coke-burning furnace

1740s   Benjamin Huntsman invents an English version of wootz steel

1750   Beginning of Industrial Revolution

1831   Michael Faraday generates electricity using iron magnets

1837   Thomas Davenport invents electric motor using iron parts

1846   John Deere makes first steel plow

1855   Henry Bessemer redesigns blast furnace to produce mild steel

1869   U.S. transcontinental railroad is completed

1874   Barbed wire patented

1883   First steel cable suspension bridge, Brooklyn Bridge

1885   First steel skyscraper, Home Insurance Building in Chicago

1900   Small electric arc process used in steel production

1913   Stainless steel invented

Glossary

bellows: an accordionlike device that produces a strong blast of air when it is squeezed

blacksmith: a person who heats iron and hammers it into objects

blast furnace: a furnace in which a powerful blast of air raises the temperature of heated metals

bloom: the lumpy mass of iron and slag that forms when iron ore is heated to about 2102°F (1150°C)

carburize: to add carbon to a substance

cast: to pour

cast iron: iron that has been liquefied and poured into a mold

chain mail: body armor made of small iron rings linked together

electromagnet: a device consisting of an iron or steel core that is magnetized by a surrounding coil that carries an electric current

forge: to shape metal by heating and then hammering it; the place where metal is forged

iron: a heavy malleable metal that rusts easily

magnet: a piece of metal, including iron and steel, that possesses the ability to attract iron

mail: a fabric made of iron rings

meteorite: a chunk of matter, often rich in iron, from outer space that forms a streak of light as it encounters the friction of Earth's atmosphere

mild steel: steel that has about 0.25 percent carbon

ore: rock that contains a valuable metal

pig iron: cast iron shaped into a large bar

quench: to harden hot steel by plunging it in water

roast: to heat iron in a way that carbon on the surface of a cast-iron object combines with oxygen

rust: a reddish coating formed on iron when it is exposed to moisture; a form of iron oxide

slag: the rocky waste material left after a metal has been separated by heat from ore

smelt: to separate metal from its ore by heat

stainless steel: nonrusting steel that has at least 10.5 percent chromium to prevent corrosion

steel: iron that has had carbon added to it

temper: to reheat carburized steel in order to make it more flexible

weld: to join pieces of metal by heating them

wootz steel: a valuable steel made in India in crucibles

wrought iron: iron almost entirely free of carbon that has been heated in a furnace and hammered

For More Information

BOOKS

Aitchison, Leslie. *A History of Metals*. New York: Interscience Publishers, 1960.

Fitzgerald, Karen. *The Story of Iron*. Danbury, CT: Franklin Watts, 1997.

Langley, Andrew. *Steel*. Detroit, MI: Thomson Learning, 1993.

Raymond, Robert. *Out of the Fiery Furnace: The Impact of Metals on the History of Mankind*. University Park: Pennsylvania State University Press, 1986.

WEB SITES

orb.rhodes.edu/encyclop/culture/scitech/iron_steel.html
This site has information about iron and steel in the Middle Ages.

www.swanseahistoryweb.org.uk/subheads/ironint.htm
This site concerns iron making in Wales, but has a lot of good general information about the Industrial Age in Britain.

www.howstuffworks.com
Search this site for more information about skyscrapers and how iron and steel are made.

www.recycle-steel.org/
This is the site of the Steel Recycling Institute.

www.steel.org/learning
This is an American Iron and Steel Institute site.

Index

Page numbers in *italics* refer to illustrations.

ABOUT THE AUTHOR

Ruth G. Kassinger is a writer, teacher, and consultant. She has written books on the U.S. census and on the history and science of inventions. She also writes articles on science and technology for *The Washington Post* and *Science Weekly*. She lives outside Washington with her husband, three daughters, and a small white dog.